HISTORIC ICONS

#THEWORLDNEEDSCOLOR

African-American Pioneers Who Helped Lead the Way

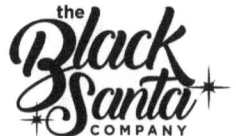

CREATIVE DIRECTOR: BARON DAVIS

WRITTEN BY: CARL REID

ILLUSTRATIONS BY: BILL MAUS

COVER DESIGN: ROSHAWN ALLEN

EDITOR: TINA DAVAR

HISTORIC ICONS: #THEWORLDNEEDSCOLOR

Volume II. Published by THE BLACK SANTA COMPANY LLC. Office of Publication 2140 Stewart Street, Santa Monica, California, USA. Copyright © 2017 THE BLACK SANTA COMPANY LLC. All prominent characters featured in this book appear by permission. The Black Santa iconography is a Trademark of THE BLACK SANTA COMPANY LLC. All Rights Reserved. No Portion of this book may be used or reproduced by any means (digital or print) without prior written permission from THE BLACK SANTA COMPANY LLC. Except for review purposes. All inquiries regarding publication rights outside the U.S., Canada, or the U.K. should be forwarded to elves@blacksanta.com.

JAMES WELDON JOHNSON
June 17, 1871 – June 26, 1938

A major figure in the Harlem Renaissance (1918-1935), James Weldon Johnson was, himself, a Renaissance man. Along with being the first black executive secretary of the NAACP, he was poet, novelist, civil rights activist, songwriter, diplomat, lawyer, and educator. He initially wrote "Lift Every Voice and Sing" in 1899 as a poem. After the inspirational poem was set to music by Johnson's brother, it became known as "The Negro National Anthem" and was adopted as the official song of the NAACP. "Lift Every Voice and Sing" would go on to become a signature song of the African-American Civil Rights movement.

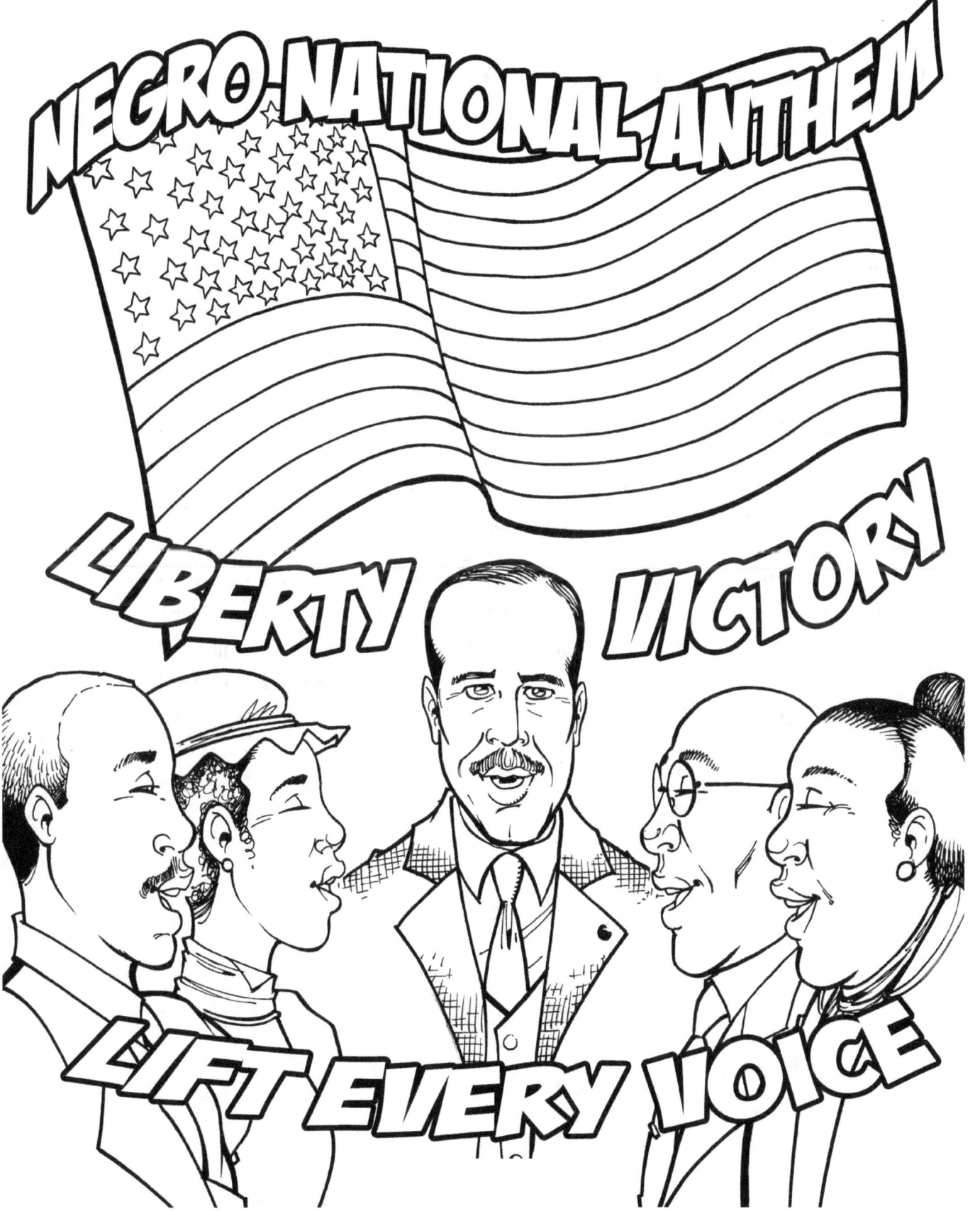

DANIEL HALE WILLIAMS
January 18, 1856 – August 4, 1931

Daniel Hale Williams was a brilliant surgeon who, on July 10th, 1893, performed the second successful pericardial heart surgery, saving a man's life. The surgery took place at Dr. Williams' own hospital, Provident Hospital, which he was forced to found upon graduating medical school, as black doctors were not allowed to work in Chicago hospitals at the time.

The night before the surgery, a man named James Cornish had walked into Provident with a knife wound to his chest. After determining that an operation was needed when the bleeding refused to stop, Dr. Williams and his fellow surgeon, Dr. Henry Dalton, pioneered a technique that created a "window" in the heart's tissue that gave the doctors enough access to directly repair the wound. Today, this is a common technique in open heart surgery that has helped save countless lives.

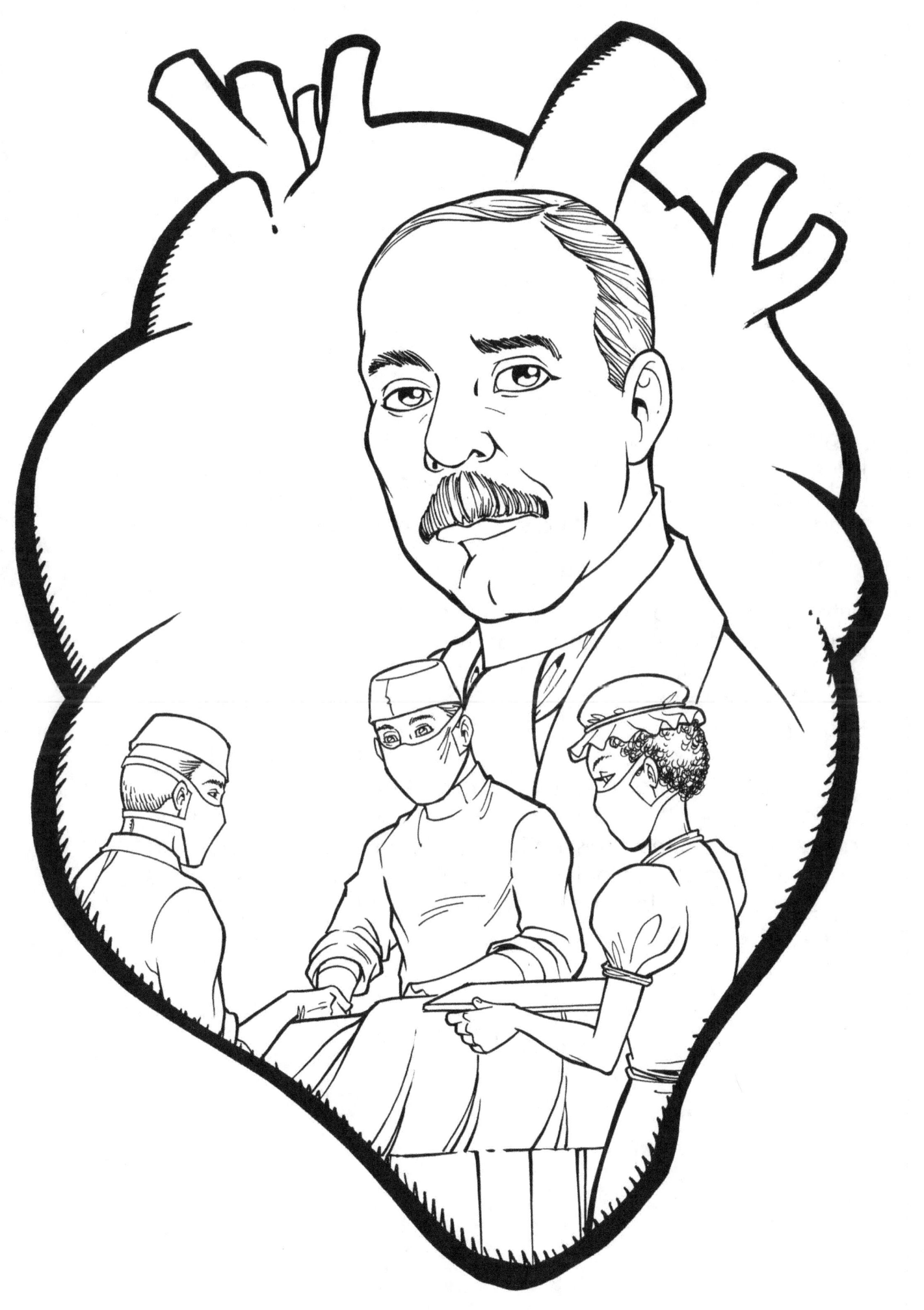

GOOSE TATUM
May 31, 1921 – January 18, 1967

A gifted professional athlete in both baseball and basketball, Reece "Goose" Tatum was best known for his time as a Harlem Globetrotter All-Star, where his comedic antics on the court made him a fan-favorite and earned him the title of the team's "Clown Prince."

With a wingspan of 84 inches and standing 6'4", Goose Tatum played with the Globetrotters for twelve seasons and is generally credited with being the inventor of the hook shot. For his contributions to the sport, Goose Tatum was inducted into the Basketball Hall of Fame in 2011.

But even while his basketball career ascended, Tatum continued to play first base with various professional Negro League teams, including the Louisville Black Colonels, the Memphis Red Sox, the Birmingham Black Barons, and the Indianapolis Clowns — never abandoning his love for the great American pastime.

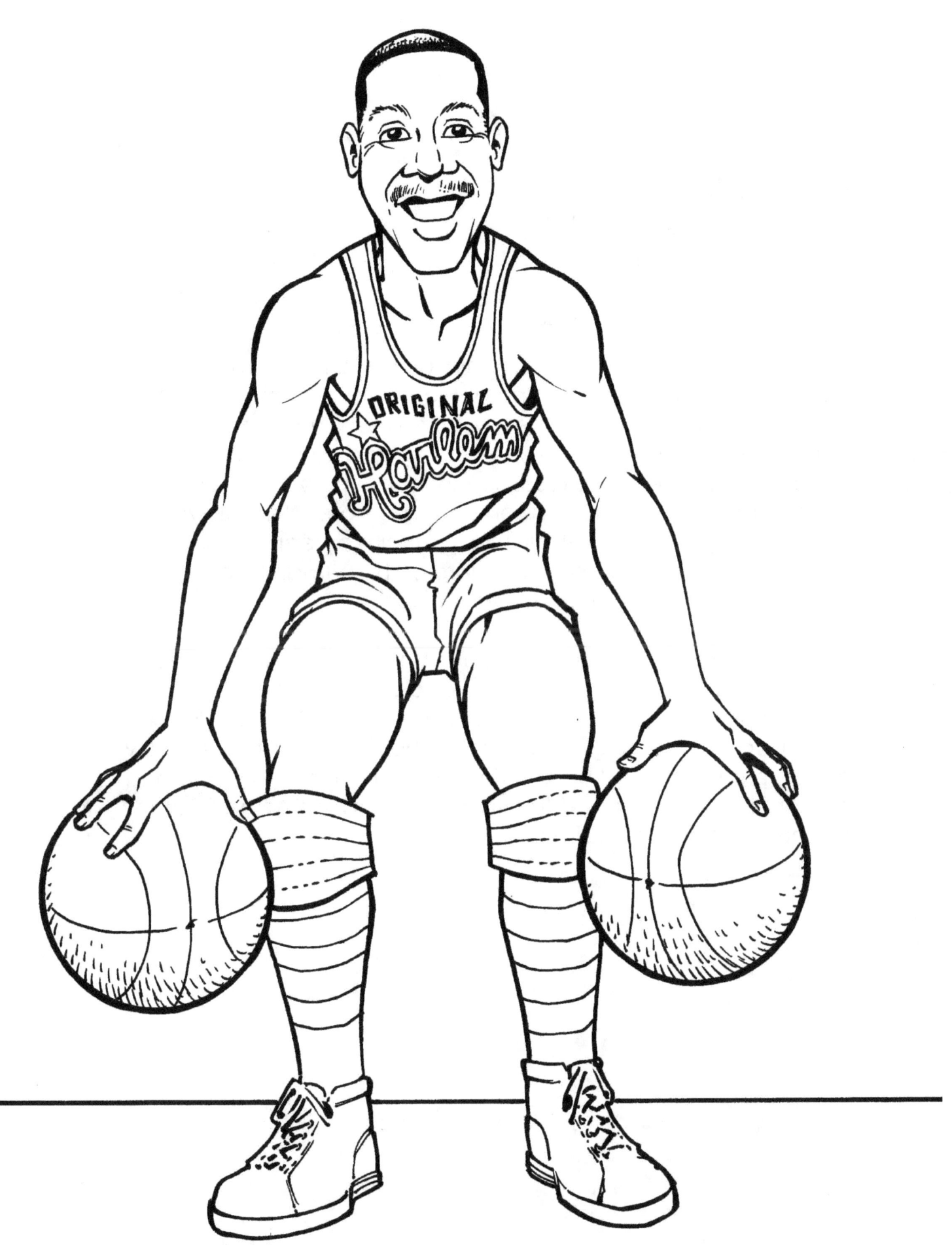

ERNIE BARNES
July 15 1938 – April 27, 2009

A multi-dimensional man of many talents, Ernie Barnes was a professional football player and one of the most popular artists in the world. After playing in the NFL for five seasons, Barnes quit to paint full-time. His distinct style of elongated figures rendered in dynamic poses became a sensation for its ability to capture the vibrancy of black culture in art. Barnes noted that it was his study of the game of football that gave him a deeper appreciation of the power, form, and structure of the human body, which would be key to his painting later on.

Barnes' paintings have been featured in countless films and television shows throughout the years, and even more copies of his masterworks hang proudly on the walls of black households. His most popular painting, "The Sugar Shack," depicting a lively dance club, was used by Marvin Gaye for an album cover and also on the "Good Times" television show, which helped Barnes become a global sensation.

Ernie Barnes Did not want people to limit themselves to drawing within the lines. We invite you to express your creativity for Ernie in the space above.

CRISPUS ATTUCKS
Circa 1723 – March 5, 1770

Crispus Attucks was a Revolutionary martyr. He was the first to fall during the Boston Massacre, a key event that led to the American Revolutionary War. On March 5, 1770, a group of colonists defended a boy who claimed a British soldier had refused to pay a barber bill. The colonists threw snowballs at the British soldiers, who eventually opened fire, killing five people, including Attucks.

In the Massacre's aftermath, tensions between the British and colonists grew. In time, the colonists would band together and spark the Revolutionary War, a struggle that led to the formation of the United States of America. Crispus exemplified values of liberty and justice in standing against oppression that would become founding tenets of this great nation.

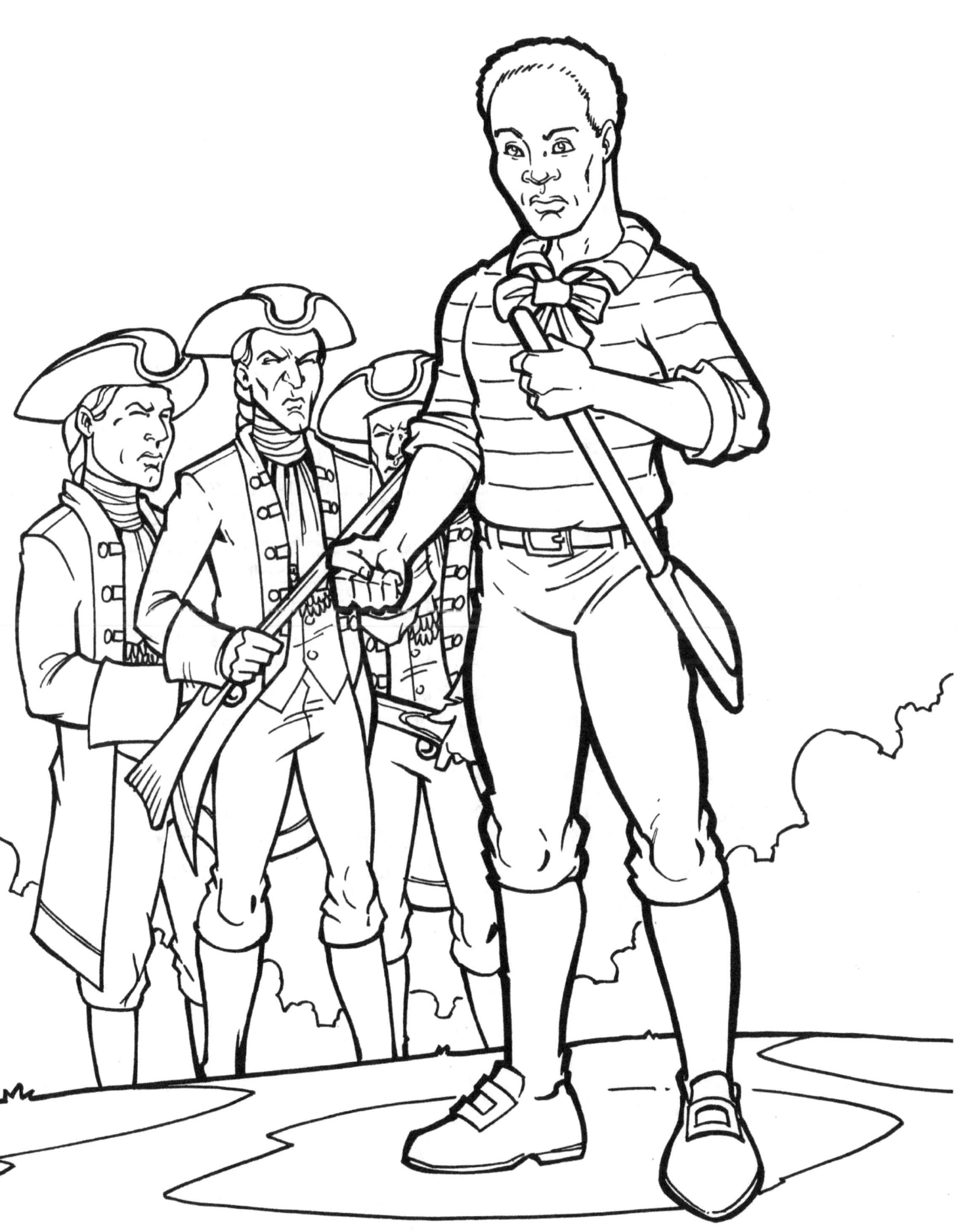

ROBERT S. ABBOTT
November 24, 1870 – February 29, 1940

The founder of THE CHICAGO DEFENDER newspaper, which would come to have the widest circulation of any black-owned newspaper in the nation, Robert Abbott was also a respected lawyer and social reform activist. In 1905, Abbott published 300 copies of the first issue of THE DEFENDER from a spare room in his boardinghouse, which he then sold door to door. He got into journalism out of a desire to promote social justice for black people. THE DEFENDER fought for political and economic equality. It attacked discrimination and segregation. The daily newspaper is credited with alerting African-Americans in the still-segregated South to the job opportunities in northern cities like Chicago, spurring a migration north which ultimately numbered in the hundreds of thousands.

A pivotal figure in Chicago's history, Abbott would also go on to co-found the Bud Billiken Parade and Picnic in 1929, which remains, to this day, a celebration of black achievement every year in the "Windy City."

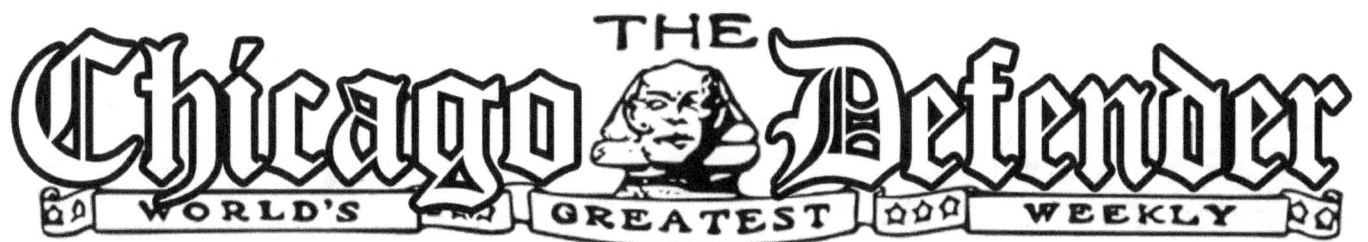

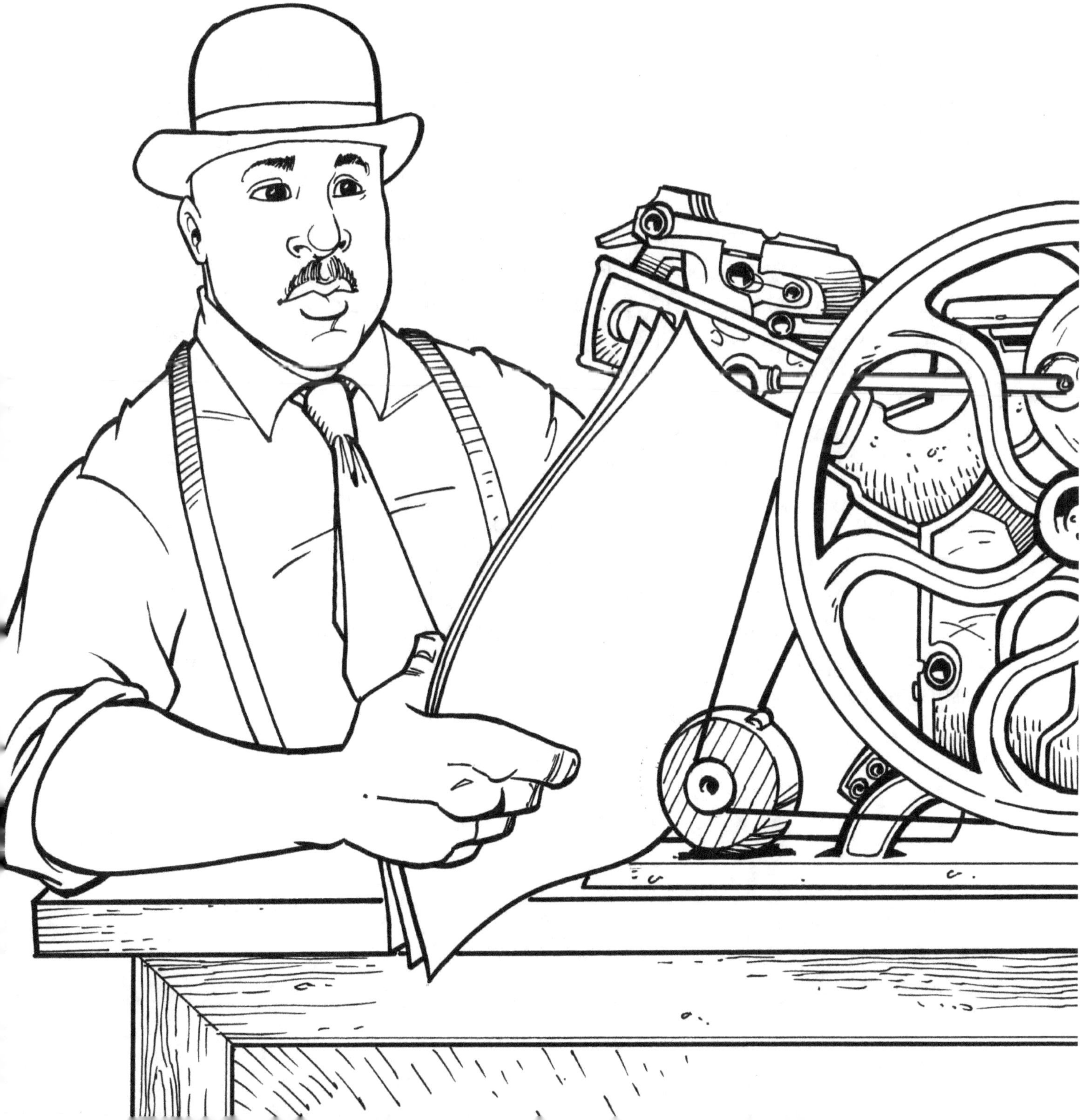

BESSIE COLEMAN
January 26, 1892 – April 30, 1926

Bessie Coleman was the first black female airplane pilot and the first woman of Native American descent to acquire a pilot's license. She was the first of both backgrounds to hold an international pilot's license, as well. While working as a manicurist in Chicago, Bessie heard amazing stories from former WWI pilots that sparked her fascination with taking to the skies. However, no American flight schools would train black people or women at the time. Headstrong and determined, Bessie took a French-language course at the Berlitz school in Chicago and then traveled to Paris in 1920, where she gained her pilot's license.

But to make a living as a pilot back then, before commercial airlines existed, Bessie knew she would need to become a "barnstormer" stunt pilot, performing dazzling aerial tricks at aviation shows. She returned to Europe, training under stunt masters in France, the Netherlands, and Germany, then returned to take America by storm as "Queen Bess," one of the air's most daring and thrilling spectacles. Tragically, Bessie lost her life in a plane crash as a passenger. She was only thirty-four years old at the time of her passing.

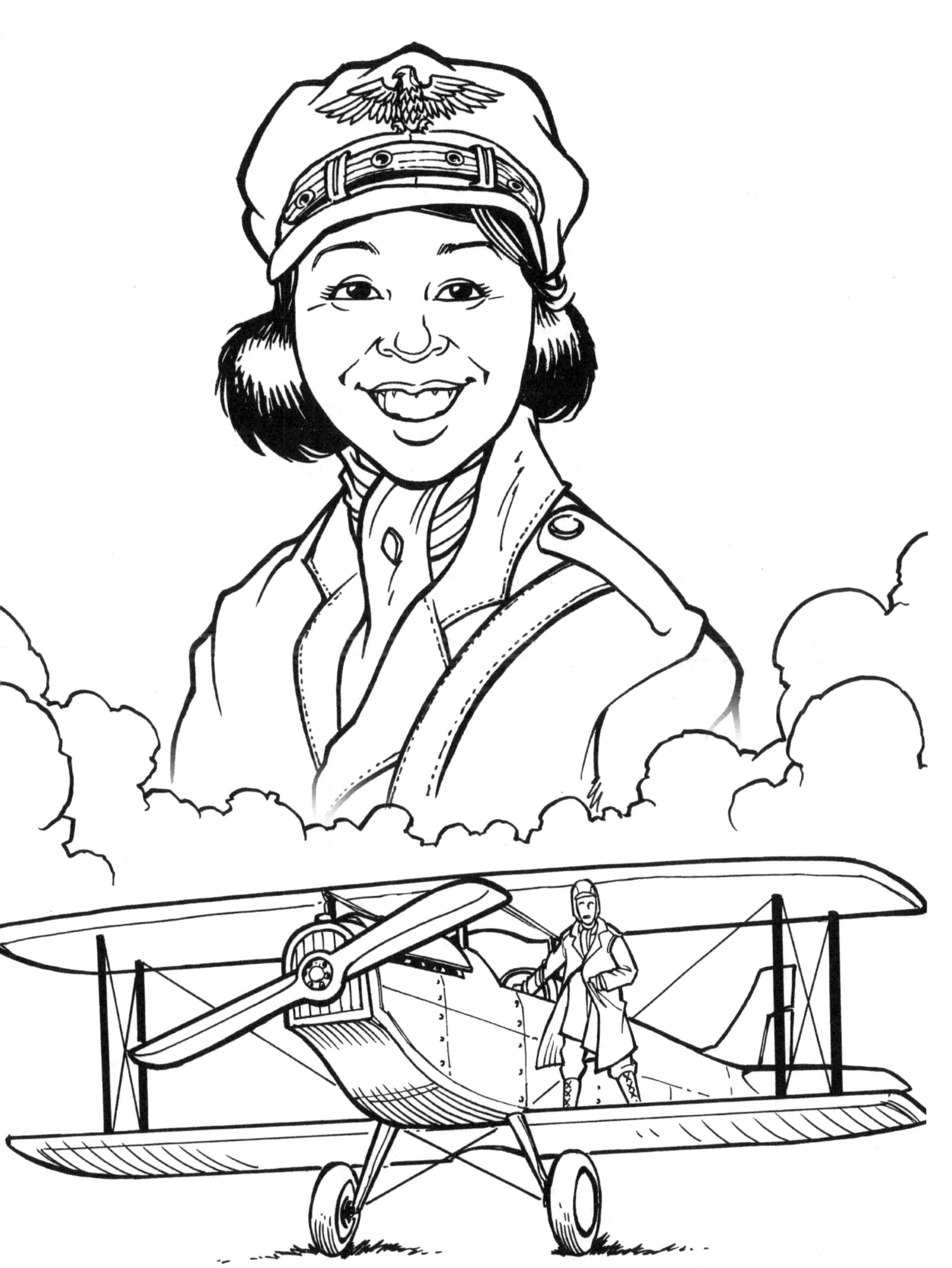

MATTHEW HENSON
August 8, 1866 – March 9, 1955

Matthew Henson was a modern-day explorer and the first black man to ever reach the Arctic Circle. Over the course of almost twenty-three years, he made seven expeditions to the Arctic with fellow explorer, Robert Peary. Henson served as the trip's navigator, craftsman, and conduit to the area's Inuit people, learning their language and trading with them to acquire key provisions for their missions.

In 1909, these men planted the American flag within five miles of the North Pole, and for that achievement, Henson became the first black man invited into The Explorer's Club in 1937.

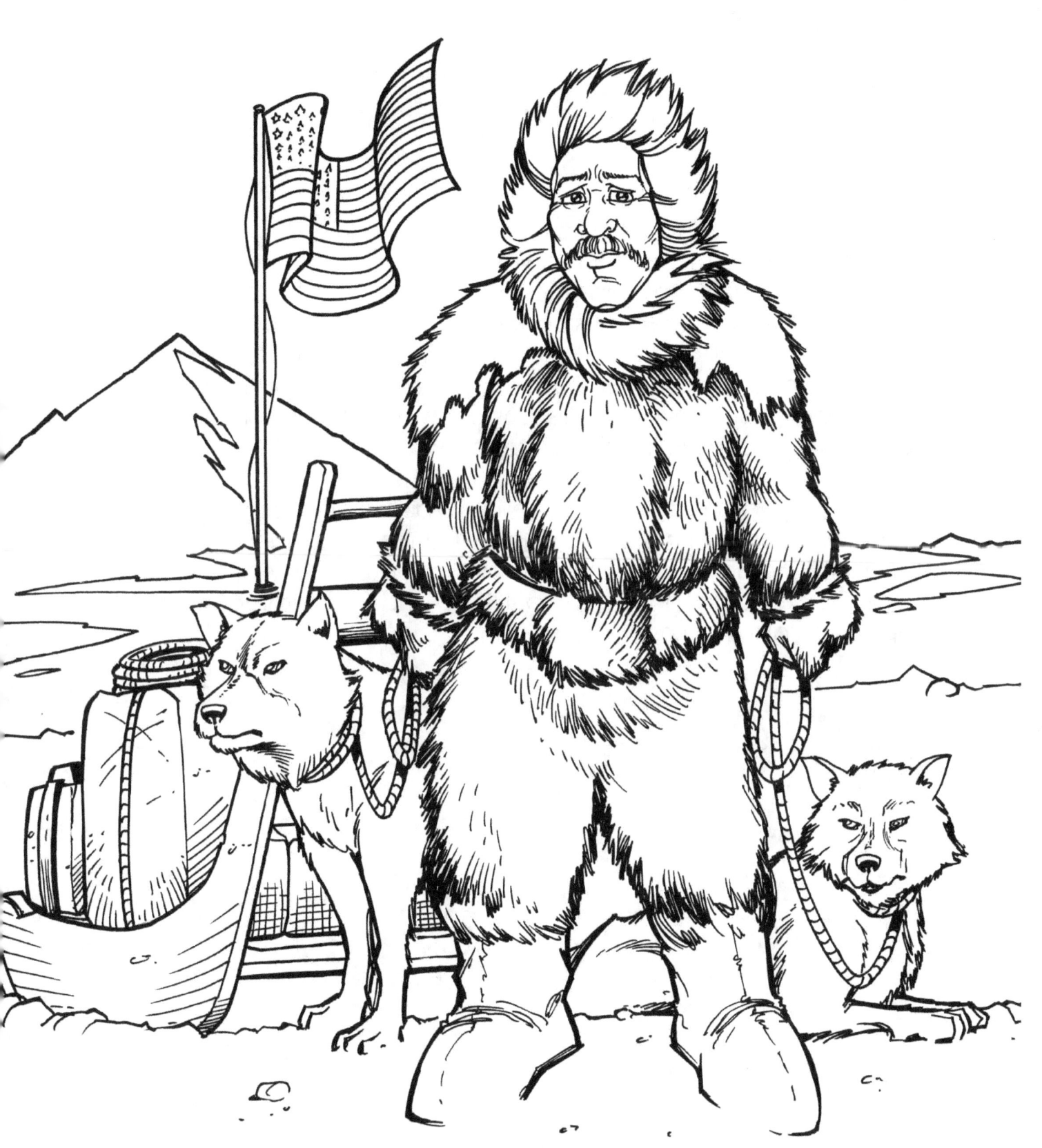

ROGER TROUTMAN
November 29, 1951 – April 25, 1999

A pioneer of the musical "funk wave" and a huge influence on the original, West Coast hip-hop sound, Roger Troutman (known simply as "Roger") was a musical legend. A songwriter, producer, composer, as well as a virtuoso on the guitar, keyboard, harmonica, flute, and vibraphone, Roger was the founder of the band Zapp and best known for his custom-made "Golden Throat" talkbox that gave him his signature sound.

Roger Troutman had four gold-selling albums with Zapp, which included the mega-hits, "Be Alright," "Dance Floor," and "Heartbreaker." Samples of his music have been used by everyone from Prince to Snoop Dogg to NWA, and most famously, in Tupac's "California Love."

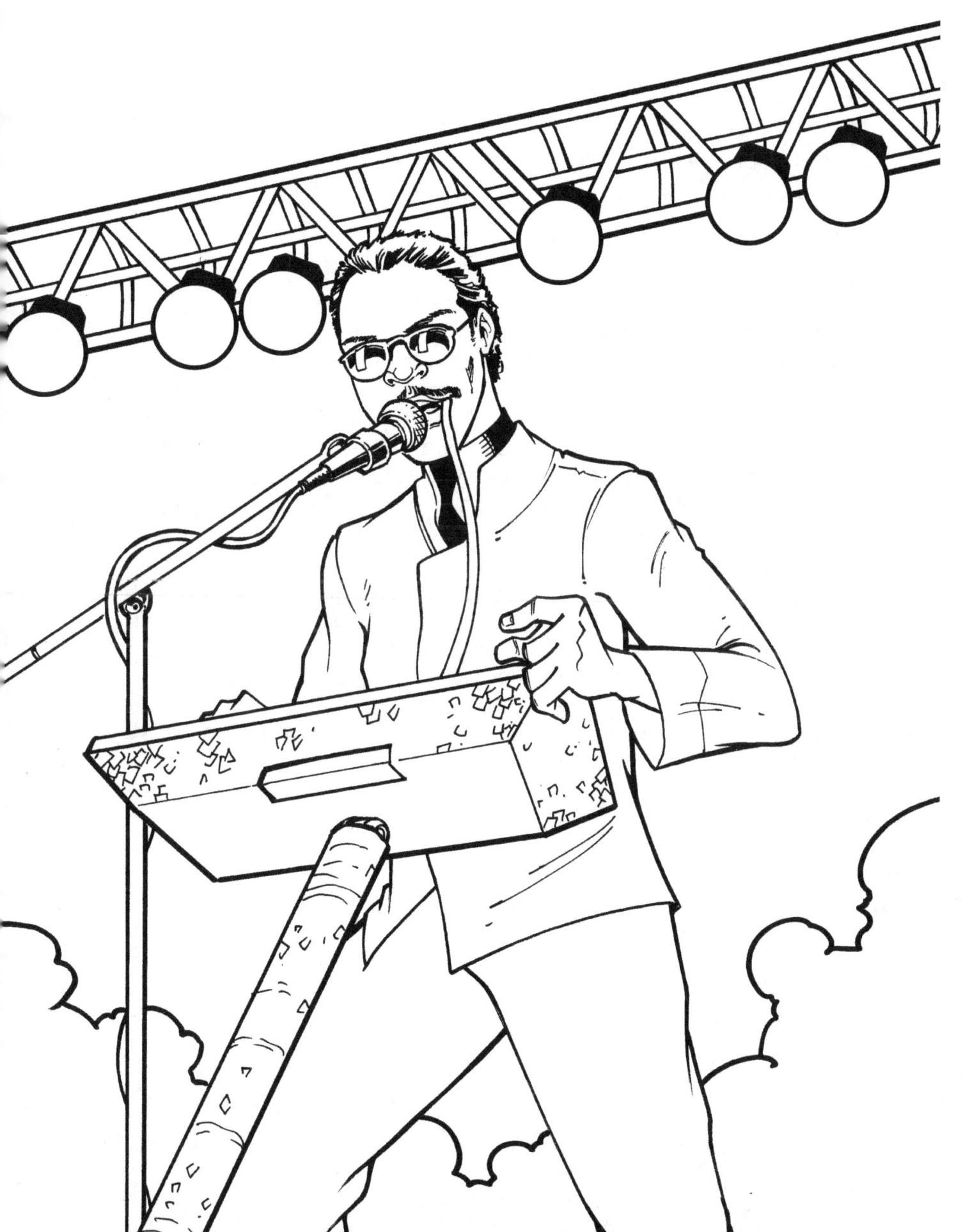

SCOTT JOPLIN
C. 1867/68 – April 1, 1917

Dubbed the "King of Ragtime," Scott Joplin was an early 20th century composer and gifted piano player credited as being a major pioneer of ragtime music. Ragtime is a style of piano music characterized by "ragged," syncopated rhythms and a lively tempo. Joplin's early piece, "Maple Leaf Rag," published in 1899, became the genre's biggest and most influential hit, setting off a national ragtime craze that lasted until Joplin's death in 1917.

"Maple Leaf Rag" remains a popular and timeless piece of music to this day, as Joplin's legacy endures to inspire new generations of talented musicians. For his legacy on the musical landscape, Scott Joplin received a posthumous Pulitzer Prize in 1976.

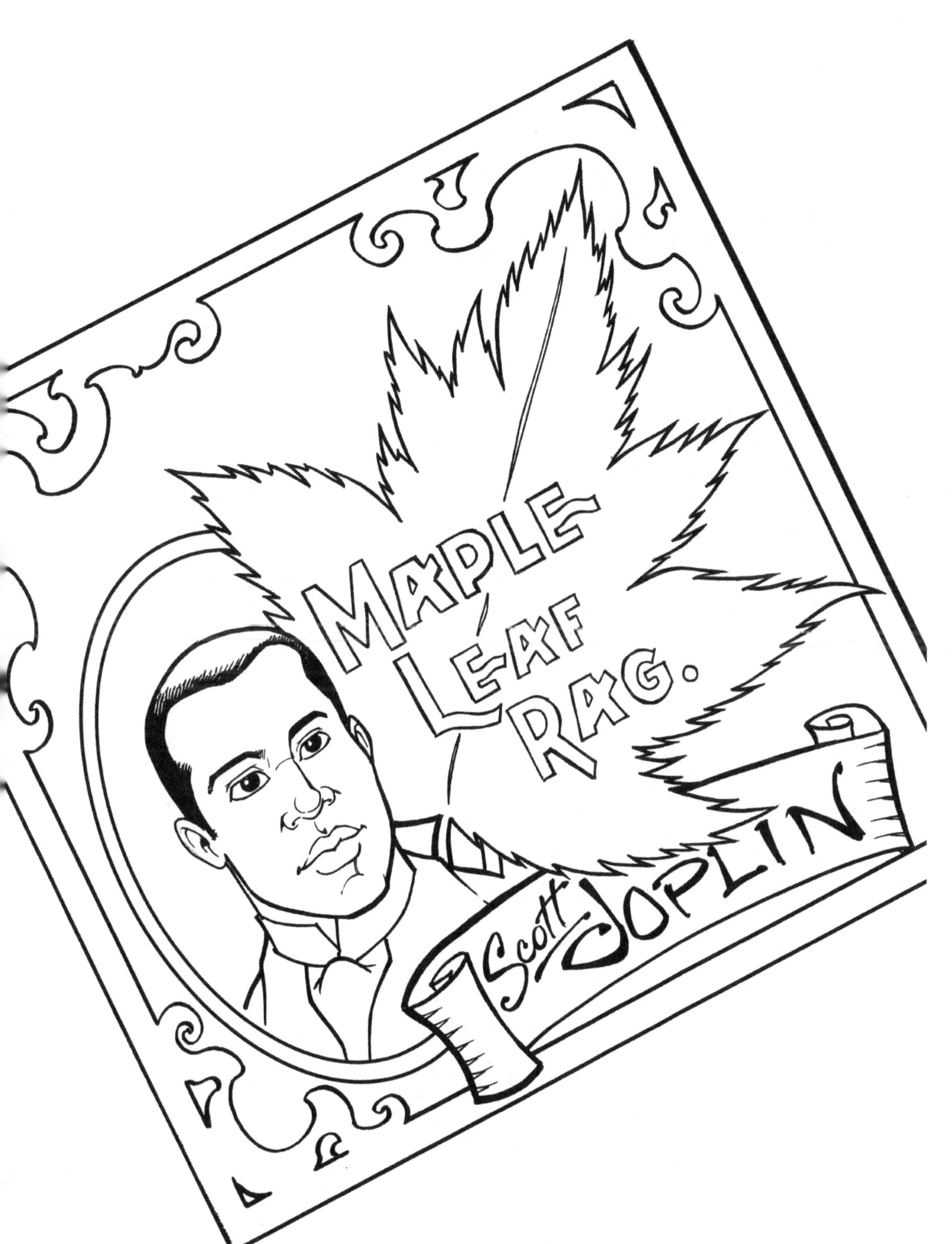

JACK JOHNSON
March 31, 1878 – June 10, 1946

The "Galveston Giant" became the first African-American world heavyweight boxing champion in 1908. After advancing his way through the "black only" boxing leagues, Johnson overcame the prejudice and discrimination of his era to break the color barrier that prevented black people from fighting for the world title.

Johnson was a dominant boxer, often toying with opponents in a flashy style that amused the crowds. He was crowned world champion for eight consecutive years, and Johnson remains an example of one of the very first sports celebrities.

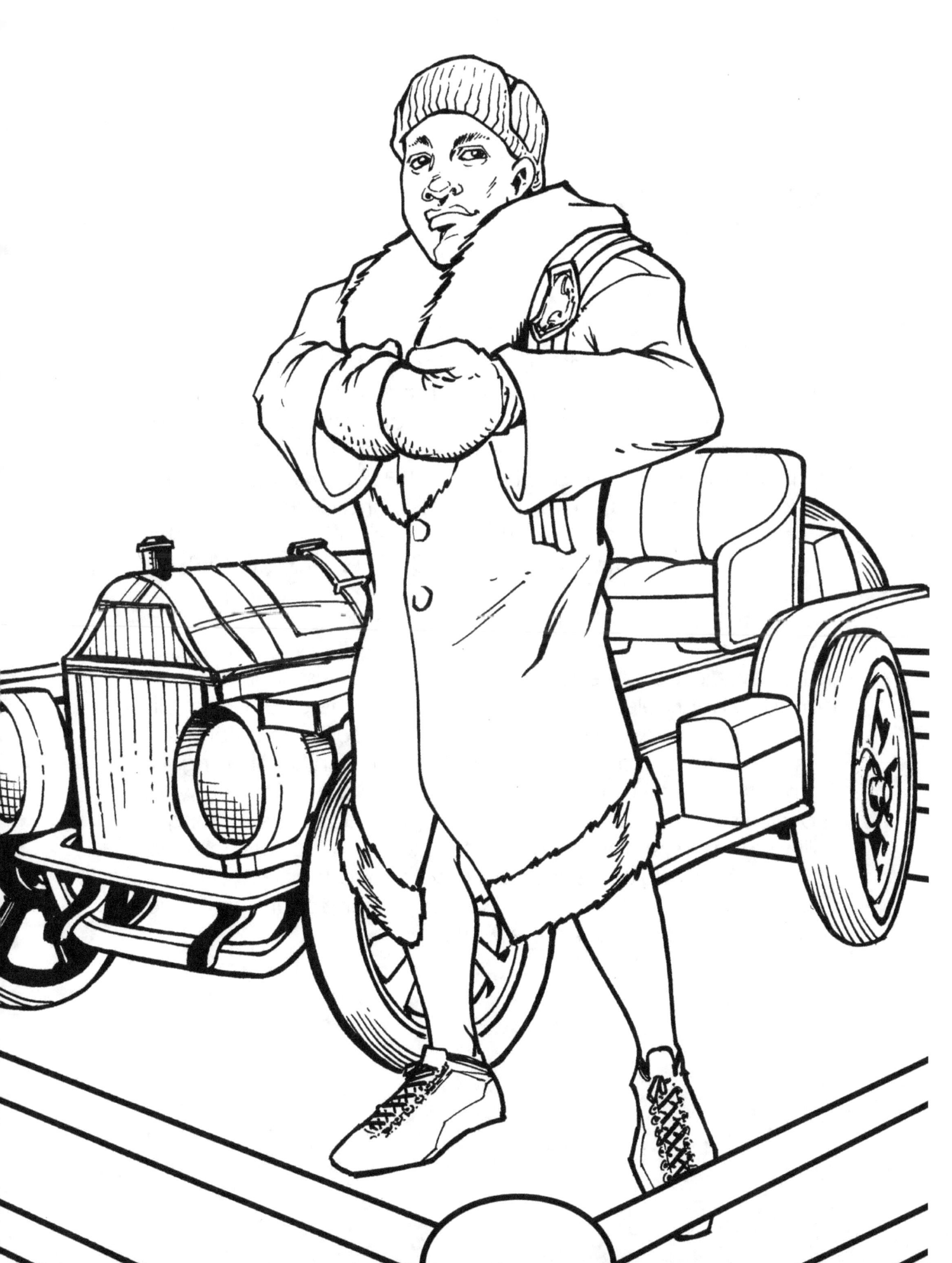

EMORY DOUGLAS
B. May 24, 1943

Emory Douglas is an artist and political activist who served as Minister of Culture for the Black Panthers from 1967 until the party disbanded in the '80s. Emory's artwork, with its strong, black lines and emotive, impressionistic undertones, was high-lighted in most issues of THE BLACK PANTHER newspaper, where Douglas was main illustrator, art director, and designer. Follow-ing that paper's run, he worked for over thirty years at the black community focused SAN FRANCISCO SUN REPORTER.

During the height of the Civil Rights movement, Douglas' imagery depicting the African-American struggle for social justice would become iconic, with many of his original works considered priceless today. Emory's art helped boost his paper's popularity and circulate its call for political action, gal-vanizing the people to come together and fight for their rights. Rather than portraying the disenfranchised as victims, his work typically showed the anger and outrage of a people no longer willing to take systematic abuse lying down. A leader then and now, Emory Douglas is still an advocate for change and politi-cal justice. He continues to make new art and share his iconic work in exhibitions around the world.

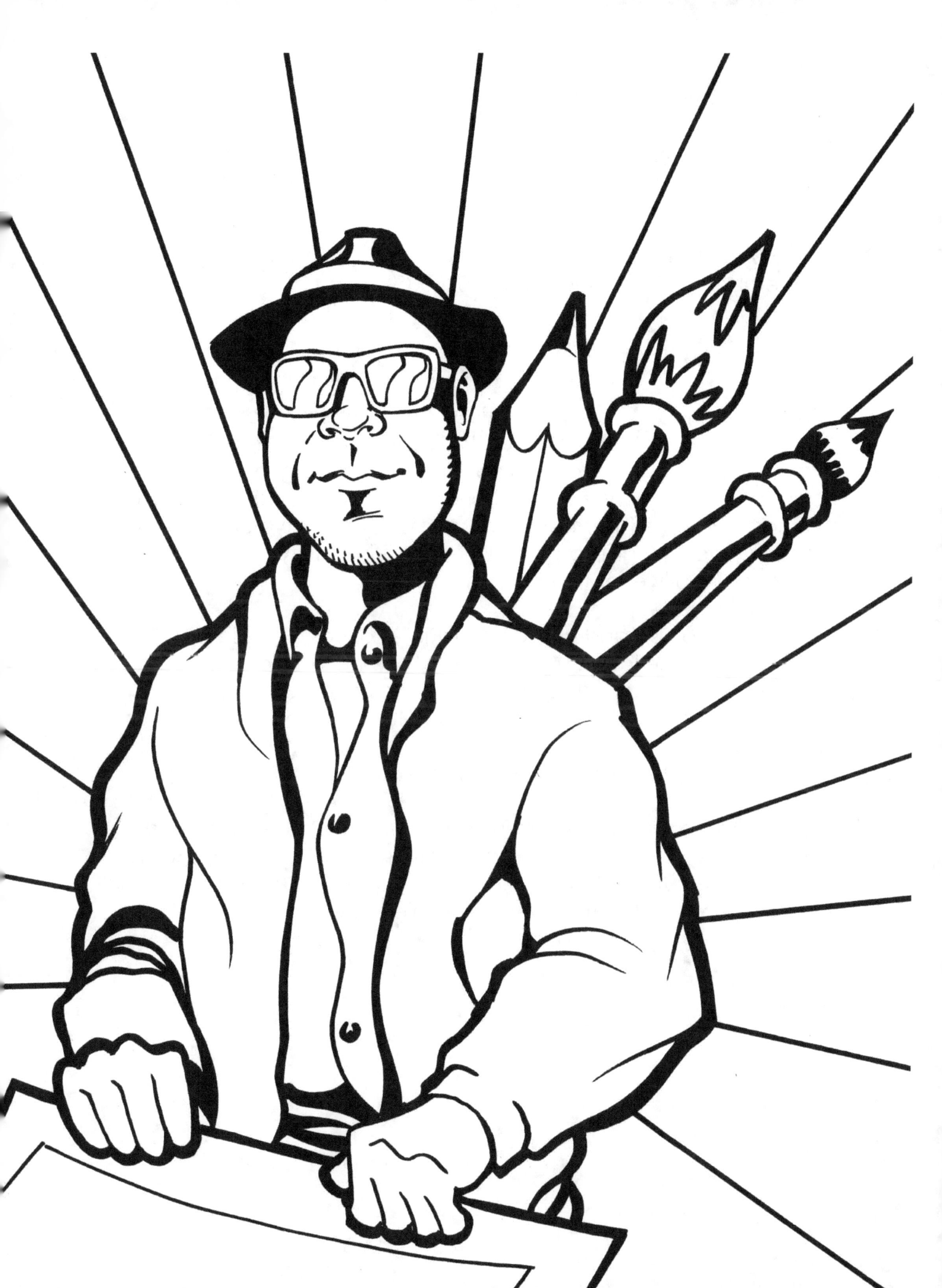

RICHARD PRYOR
December 1, 1940 – December 10, 2005

Known for his astute and hilarious social observations and his razor-sharp insight on racial and topical issues of the era, Richard Pryor was, simply, a comedy legend. Possessing an unrivaled ability to tell a story in gut-busting and often profane fashion, Richard achieved tremendous success for the atypical level of intimacy he brought to his routines, crafting a style that would influence nearly every comic to follow him.

In addition to his stand-up acclaim, Richard was a staple in Hollywood during the late '70s and '80s, where he signed a five-year, $40 million contract with Columbia Pictures and starred in such hit films as *Silver Streak, Car Wash, The Muppet Movie, Stir Crazy, Bustin' Loose, The Toy, and Brewster's Millions,* along with co-writing the comedy classic, *Blazing Saddles.*

In 1998, Richard received the initial Mark Twain Prize for American Humor. He co-hosted the Academy Awards twice and won three consecutive Grammys for Best Comedy Recording from 1975-1977, as well as their Lifetime Achievement Award in 2006.

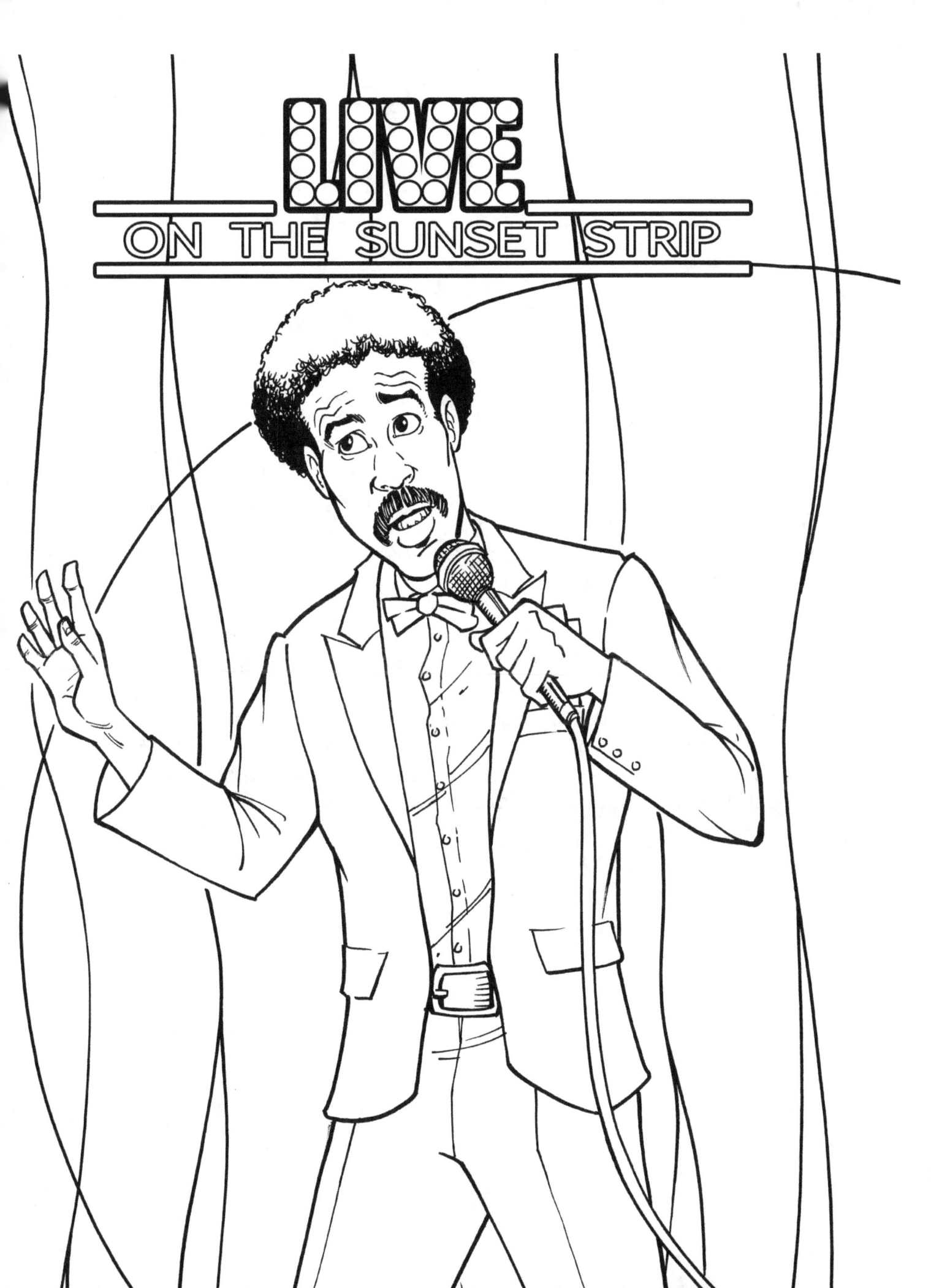

SAMUEL BATTLE
January 16, 1883 – August 7, 1966

Sworn in on March 6, 1911, Samuel Battle was the first African-American to serve as a New York City police officer. While working as a train porter, Battle began studying for the police department civil service exam. After working his way through the ranks, he later became the first New York City black police sergeant in 1926, the first black lieutenant in 1935, and the first black parole commissioner in 1941.

Battle initially oversaw the Manhattan neighborhood where Lincoln Center is today. He later transferred to Harlem as New York City's black population continued to grow. Samuel Battle became instrumental in quelling racial tensions in Harlem, taking proactive steps to help stop the violence of the 1935 Harlem Riots and during the race riot of 1943 after a white police officer shot an African-American soldier.

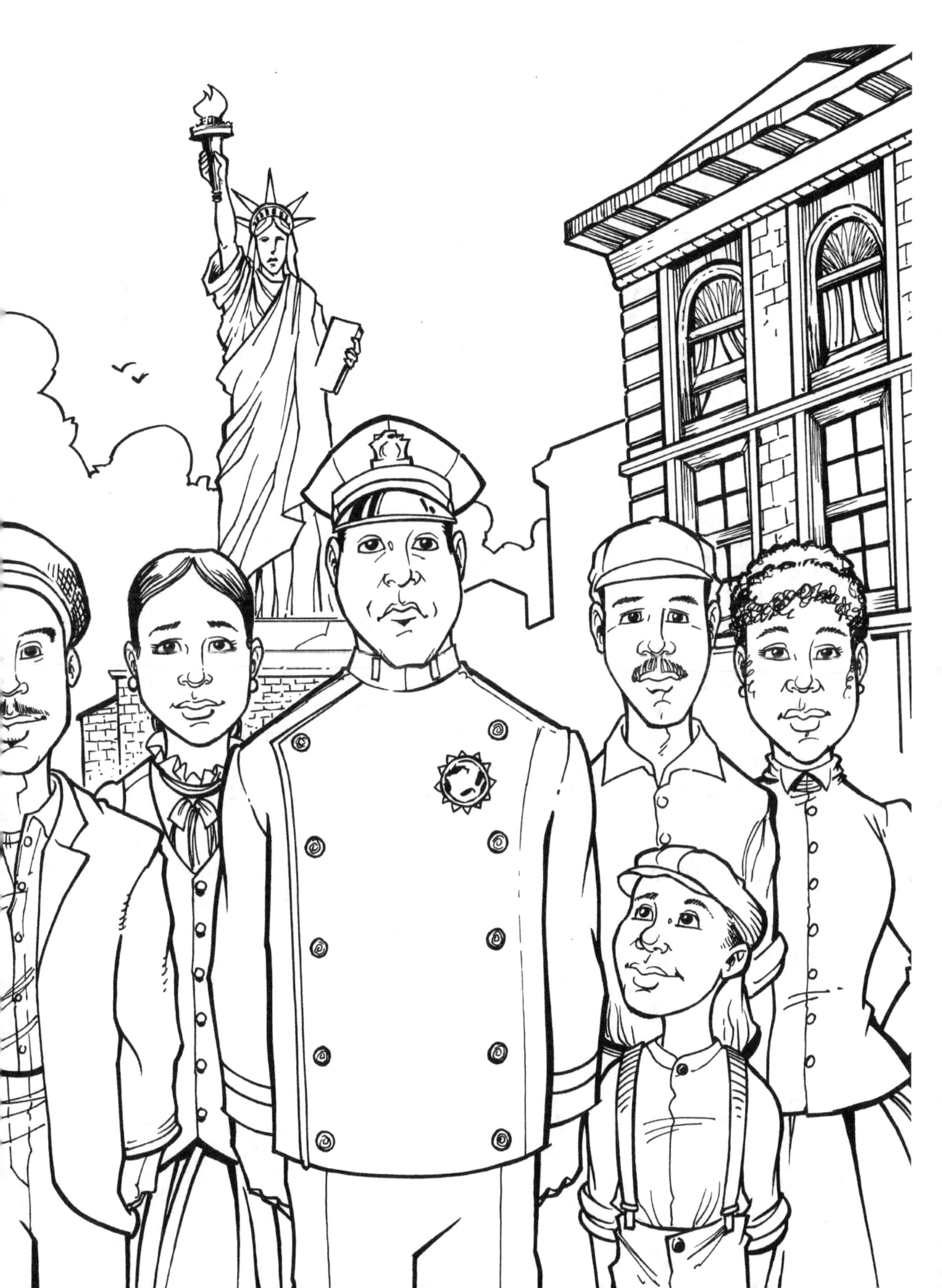

THE OBAMAS

The first black First Family of the United States, President Barack Obama, First Lady Michelle Obama, and daughters Malia and Sasha Obama are prime examples of an accomplished, loving family for not only the African-American community, but families worldwide.

During his eight years as America's 44th president, Mr. Obama oversaw the country's rescue from economic collapse, the resuscitation of the housing and financial markets and the American auto industry, and the implementation of regulations on reckless Wall Street trading; created the Consumer Protection Bureau; effected passage of the Affordable Care Act; spurred a green energy revolution; reached a world-changing climate deal with China and nineteen other nations; reopened communications with Cuba; improved schools with Race to the Top and reformation of the student loan system; signed into effect landmark laws protecting LGBT citizens and women from discriminatory practices; and initiated the My Brother's Keeper program to help young men of color reach their full potential in a frequently prejudiced world.

Michelle Obama, who holds degrees from Princeton University and Harvard Law School, graduated to become an accomplished lawyer and writer. As well as being a wonderful mother, she has become an instrumental advocate for children's nutrition with her Let's Move! initiative, which helped curb childhood obesity in retooling school lunches for healthier eating options.

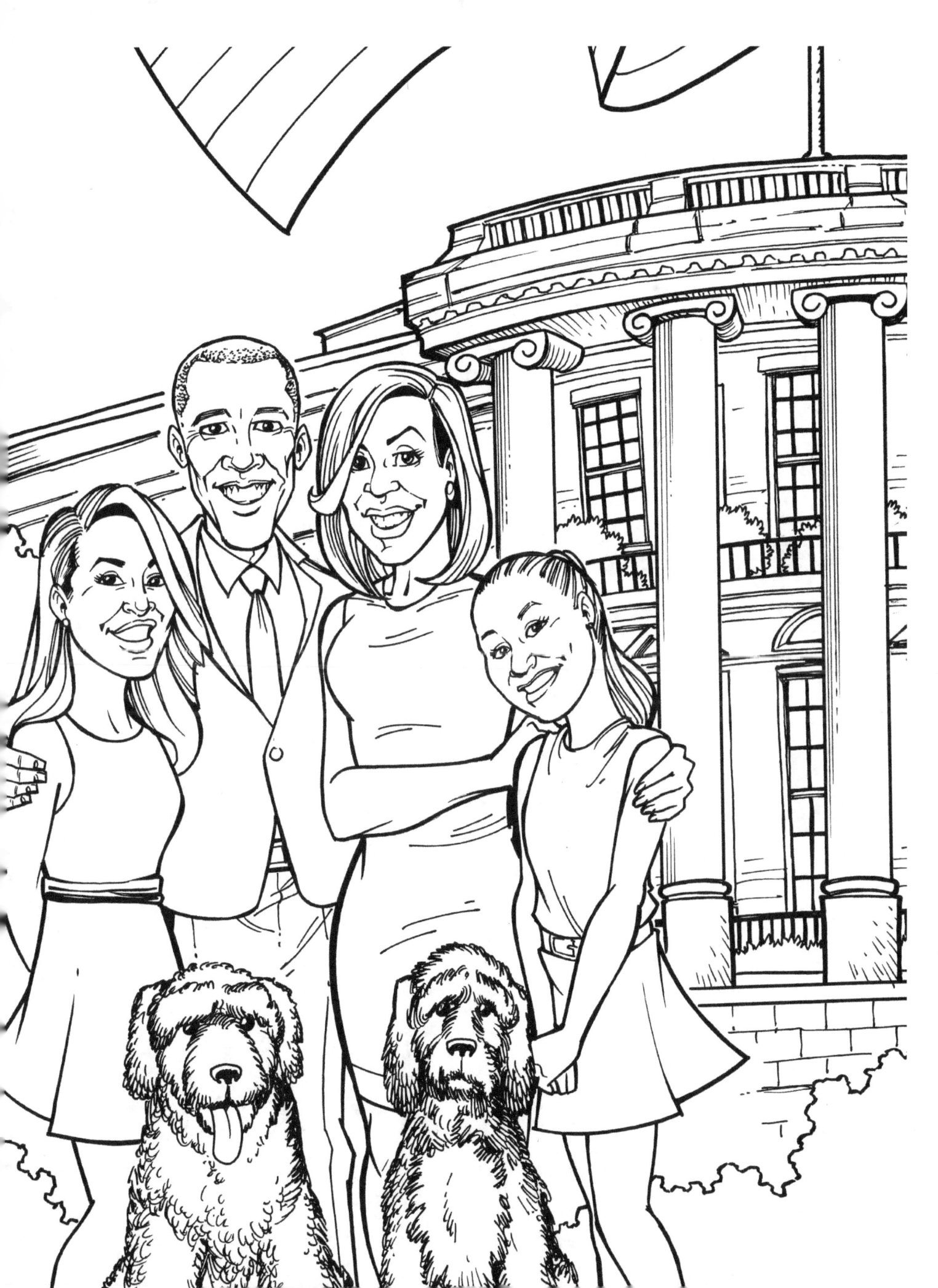

Us

The Black Santa Company's founder and principal, Baron Davis, had a highly successful thirteen year career in the National Basketball Association. An NBA All- Star and record holder, Baron played for the Charlotte Hornets, the Golden State Warriors, the Los Angeles Clippers, the Cleveland Cavaliers, and the New York Nicks. Known for his electrifying style on the court, Baron was a powerful point guard who won national acclaim for executing in crucial, high-pressure moments when his team needed him the most. As with all successful, professional athletes in team sports, their playing days end when they are still young men and women. The question for each then becomes: what next?

For Baron Davis, the answer was to bring creative talent together to develop, publish, and produce a variety of original stories with a heart and educational values that appeal to global audiences of all ages and recognize the value of diversity. This led to him founding multiple companies – Sports and Lifestyle in Culture (SLIC), No Label, and The Black Santa Company.

As an entrepreneur, investor, and businessman, Baron actively guides each of these ventures, with more to come. Additionally, Baron served as a producer of the lauded documentaries Crips and Bloods: Made in America; 30 for 30: Sole Man; and The Drew: No Excuse, Just Produce, among others. Baron is also a mentor and coach for young, upcoming basketball players and a longtime supporter of the Boys and Girls Club of Venice. His nonprofit, Rising Stars of America, established in 1999, helps to raise funds for basketball camps and sponsors AAU teams across Los Angeles.

"I started The Black Santa Company to create positive, uplifting, and educational experiences that celebrate our differences, while deepening our sense of unity and responsibility to one another."

--Baron Davis

SPECIAL THANKS to Naomi Tatum, Bernie Barnes, Diedre Barnes, Luz Rodriguez, Taji Troutman, Mercedes Livingston, Roger's Legacy LLC, Emory Douglas, Jennifer Pryor, Michael Farhat, Carl Reid, Bill Maus, Steve Stern, and Tina Davar.